LIGHTBOX

Go to **www.openlightbox.com**, and enter this book's unique code.

ACCESS CODE

LBA39435

Lightbox is an all-inclusive digital solution for the teaching and learning of curriculum topics in an original, groundbreaking way. Lightbox is based on National Curriculum Standards.

STANDARD FEATURES OF LIGHTBOX

 AUDIO High-quality narration using text-to-speech system

 ACTIVITIES Printable PDFs that can be emailed and graded

 SLIDESHOWS Pictorial overviews of key concepts

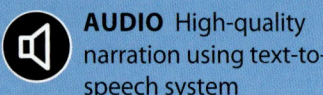 **VIDEOS** Embedded high-definition video clips

 WEBLINKS Curated links to external, child-safe resources

 TRANSPARENCIES Step-by-step layering of maps, diagrams, charts, and timelines

 INTERACTIVE MAPS Interactive maps and aerial satellite imagery

 QUIZZES Ten multiple choice questions that are automatically graded and emailed for teacher assessment

 KEY WORDS Matching key concepts to their definitions

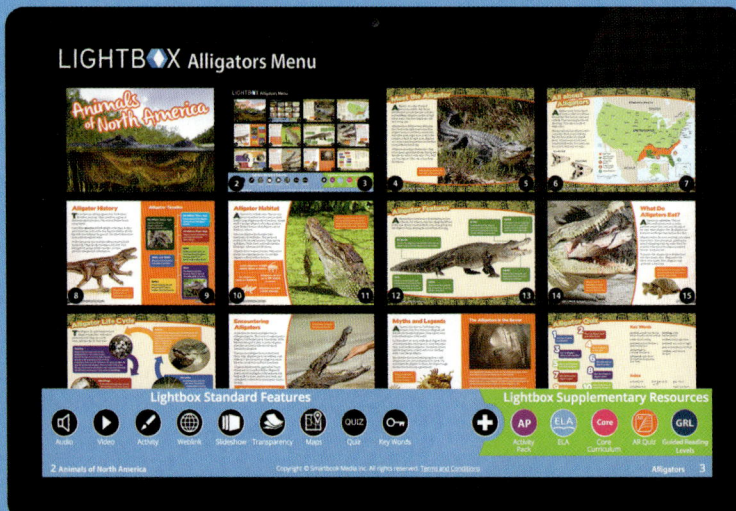

Copyright © 2016 Smartbook Media Inc. All rights reserved.

Contents

Lightbox Access Code	2
Meet the Eagle	4
All about Eagles	6
Eagle History	8
Eagle Habitat	10
Eagle Features	12
What Do Eagles Eat?	14
Eagle Life Cycle	16
Encountering Eagles	18
Myths and Legends	20
Eagle Quiz	22
Key Words/Index	23
Log on to www.openlightbox.com	24

Meet the Eagle

Eagles are birds of **prey**. These birds hunt other animals for food. Eagles are warm-blooded animals that lay eggs. They have feathers, a beak with no teeth, and a small skeleton.

Eagles are different from other birds of prey, such as owls and hawks. They are larger, heavier, and more powerful. Their hooked beaks, strong legs, and powerful **talons** make it easy for them to prey on other animals. Sharp eyesight helps them spot their prey from high above.

Eagles live in every kind of **habitat**. These include forests, wetlands, deserts, mountains, and farmlands. Eagles can also live in towns and cities with parks.

> Eagles have hollow bones that are lightweight. This helps the birds to fly.

All about Eagles

Eagles come from a family of birds called *Accipitridae*. This family includes many other birds of prey, such as hawks and kites. Eagles are divided into four groups, based on how they look and behave.

The golden eagle is the largest bird of prey in North America. They are named for their golden-brown feathers. Bald eagles get their name from their white, feathered heads. They have brown bodies, so their white heads make them look bald.

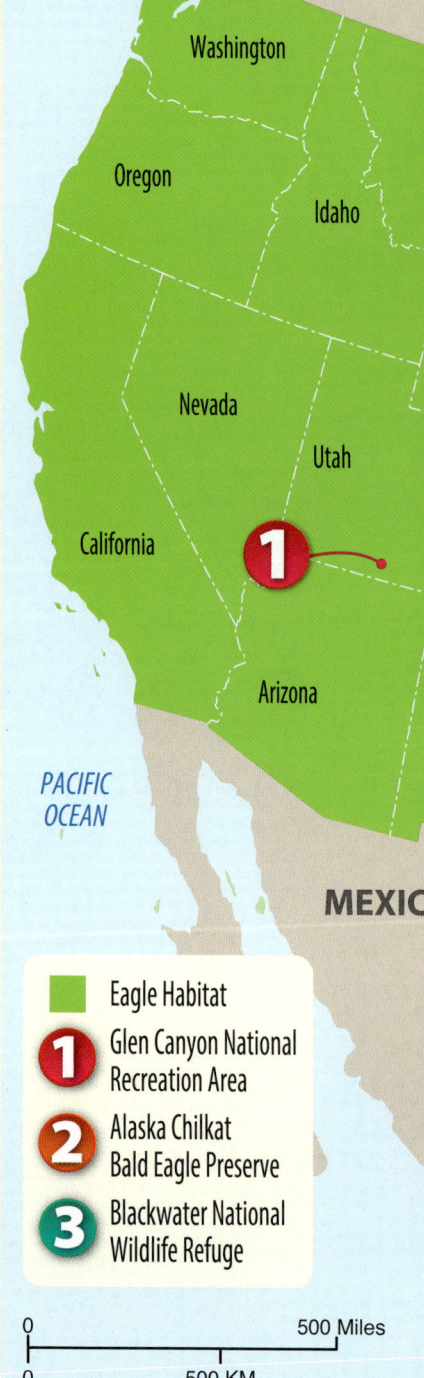

Bald Eagle

Golden Eagle

Eagle Habitat
1. Glen Canyon National Recreation Area
2. Alaska Chilkat Bald Eagle Preserve
3. Blackwater National Wildlife Refuge

Eagles in America

Eagle History

Dinosaurs are thought to be the closest relatives of birds. Today, scientists believe that birds developed from a group of meat-eating dinosaurs called theropods. Members of this group varied in size, from smaller creatures all the way up to incredibly large dinosaurs, such as the Tyrannosaurus Rex.

A combination of climate changes and natural disasters caused the dinosaurs to go **extinct**. Early birds were able to survive the changes because of their ability to fly. Humans used to train eagles to help them hunt animals. Today, this sport is known as falconry.

The Archaeopteryx, now extinct, is thought to be one of the earliest ancestors of modern birds. It looked like a cross between a bird and a small dinosaur.

Eagle Timeline

150 Million Years Ago
Archaeopteryx first appears on Earth, in the area now known as southern Germany.

1.8 Million Years Ago
The largest eagle to ever exist lives in an area now known as New Zealand. It has a 9.8-foot (3-meter) wingspan.

1782
The bald eagle is made the official bird of the United States.

1940
The U.S. Congress passes the Bald Eagle Protection Act. This act forbids killing, selling, or owning a bald eagle.

1960s
The North American bald eagle population is dangerously low. There are only 450 nesting, or breeding, pairs of bald eagles in nature. The bald eagle is listed as endangered under the Endangered **Species** Act in 1967.

August 9th, 2007
The bald eagle is removed from the United States federal list of threatened and endangered animals.

Today
There are close to 10,000 bald eagle breeding pairs in the continental U.S. The bald eagle is no longer considered an endangered species.

Eagle Habitat

Eagles are found all over the world. They live on every continent except Antarctica. The bald eagle and the golden eagle are some of the most common eagles in North America.

Eagles live in forests, mountains, and deserts. Bald eagles live near bodies of water, such as lakes and rivers. Eagles **migrate** south in winter in search of warmer climates and food supplies.

A male and a female eagle build a nest together. It is called an eyrie and is found in tall trees or on high cliffs. The nests are made of sticks and are lined with twigs, grass, and feathers. Eagles use the same nest every year. They mend the nest every spring.

To attract mates, **eagles fight** with one another and also perform **aerial tricks**.

There are **60 species** of eagles.

Golden eagles from Alaska and Canada fly south in the fall.

The bald eagle is the **only eagle** unique to **North America**.

Some eagle nests may reach 10 feet (30 m) across and weigh as much as 2,000 pounds (900 kilograms).

Eagles 11

Eagle Features

Eagle bodies are made for flying and catching prey. They have many features that help them do these tasks. For example, an eagle's feathers keep the bird warm and waterproof.

WINGS

Eagles have strong, broad wings, so they can fly high without much effort. On average, they can fly at a speed of 31 miles (50 kilometers) per hour.

TAIL

An eagle's tail feathers are very strong. Eagles use their tails to help them soar and change direction while flying. The tail also serves as a kind of brake, helping an eagle to slow down while in the air.

EARS
Eagles have ears on the sides of their heads, just behind their eyes. Feathers cover their ears, making them difficult to see.

EYES
Eagles have bright yellow eyes. Their sharp vision helps them spot their prey from a great distance. They can see clearly during the day, but not at night.

BEAK
Eagles have a large, hooked beak. It is powerful and can easily tear the flesh of prey.

LEGS
Eagles have two legs, with short, powerful toes and long talons. The sharp talons pierce prey and help hold it firmly in place.

Eagles will steal food from other eagles.

14 **Animals of North America**

What Do Eagles Eat?

Eagles are **carnivores**. This means that they mostly eat meat. Eagles hunt small animals, such as rabbits, turtles, and ducks.

Eagles swoop down from the sky to grab prey with their strong talons. The talons are razor-sharp and curved to hold prey. Eagles eat by holding prey in one claw and tearing the flesh with the other. Eagles that eat turtles will carry them to great heights and then drop the turtles onto rocks to crack open their hard shells.

Eagles can swim to the shore while carrying heavy fish. They use their wings as oars. While flying, eagles can carry prey about half their own weight.

Eagles can eat as much as 2 pounds (0.9 kg) of food at a time. A rabbit would be a large meal for an eagle.

Eagle Life Cycle

Bald eagles have one partner for most of their lives. Eagles start laying eggs when they are 4 to 5 years old. They lay eggs once a year.

Nesting
The female eagle lays between one and three eggs in the spring. Both parents care for the eggs. This includes **incubating** the eggs, hunting for food, and feeding the babies. The eggs hatch in 31 to 45 days.

Chicks
Newly hatched eagle chicks are soft and grayish-white. Their wobbly legs are too weak to hold their weight, and their eyes are partially closed. Their only protection is their parents. The older chicks grab a larger portion of the food.

16   Animals of North America

Adults

At five months, eagles are fully grown. When they are 4 or 5 years old, their eyes and beak turn yellow. The head and tail feathers change from brown to white. They have a wingspan of 6 **to** 8 feet (1.8 **to** 2.4 m). Eagles can live to be 25 years old in nature. **Captive** eagles can live as long as 50 years.

Eaglets

At four weeks, chicks are considered to be eaglets. Eaglets are brown in color. A healthy eaglet weighs 9 pounds (4 kg) at six weeks. At this time, they are nearly as large as their parents. By about three months, they are ready for **fledging**.

Eagles 17

Encountering Eagles

If you have eagles where you live, make sure that your house pets are not out at dawn or dusk. This is the time when eagles hunt. Your pets could be easy prey.

You may sometimes come face to face with an eagle. The eagle is looking for food and will not attack unless it feels it is in danger from you. If you happen to be somewhere near an eagle's nest, the mother eagle will make a noise to move you away from her nest. She is very protective of her eggs and babies.

Killing a bald eagle or a golden eagle has a **penalty** of **$10,000** and/or a year in **jail.**

In 1982, President Ronald Reagan declared January 28th National Bald Eagle Day.

Eagles can see **3.6** times **better** than a human.

Eagles usually make **nests** in trees that are more than **200** years old.

Bald eagles usually hunt fish that swim near the surface of the water.

Eagles

Myths and Legends

An old legend suggests that eagles alone have the power to look into the Sun. The Sun strengthens the eyes of eagles. According to the legend, this gives them the gift of sharp vision.

The Aztecs of Mexico respected the eagle as a strong bird. They treasured eagle feathers and often used the feathers to make headwear. Today, the golden eagle is the national bird of Mexico.

Some American Indian groups have stories about the Thunderbird, a mythical eagle. The mighty Thunderbird created thunder and lightning by clapping its wings. For this reason, eagles were both respected and feared.

The Tlingit American Indians carved the Thunderbird at the top of their totem poles.

The Myth of the Clever Eagle

According to an Aboriginal legend, at one time, eagles had very poor eyesight. However, they could fly very high. Knowing this, a king asked an eagle to watch for enemies that might harm the kingdom.

Wanting to be of help, the eagle asked a slug for his eyesight, which was very sharp. The kind slug agreed. Later, the eagle refused to return the slug's eyesight. This is how eagles developed such good vision.

Eagle Quiz

1 What time of day do eagles tend to hunt?

2 What day of the year is National Bald Eagle Day?

3 Are eagles cold-blooded or warm-blooded animals?

4 What family of birds do eagles come from?

5 What is the largest bird of prey in North America?

6 How many species of eagles are there?

7 What is the earliest ancestor of modern birds?

8 What is the average speed of an eagle?

9 What is the name of the nest that a male and female eagle build together?

10 When were bald eagles removed from the list of endangered animals in the United States?

Answers: 1. Dawn and dusk 2. January 28th 3. Warm-blooded 4. Accipitridae 5. The golden eagle 6. 60 7. Archaeopteryx 8. 31 miles per hour (50 km per hour) 9. An eyrie 10. August 9th, 2007

Animals of North America

Key Words

captive: kept in a confined space

carnivores: animals that eat meat

extinct: no longer in existence

fledging: first flight of an eaglet

habitat: natural living place

incubating: sitting on eggs for the purpose of hatching

migrate: shift from one place to another

prey: an animal hunted for food

species: a group of animals or plants that have many features in common

talons: long nails on the claws of an eagle

Index

Archaeopteryx 8, 9, 22

bald eagle 6, 9, 10, 16, 18, 19, 22

chicks 16, 17

dinosaurs 8

eaglets 17
eyesight 4, 21
eyrie 10, 22

feathers 4, 6, 10, 12, 13, 17, 20

golden eagle 6, 10, 18, 20, 22

nests 10, 11, 18, 22

talons 4, 13, 15

Eagles

LIGHTB⬥X

➕ SUPPLEMENTARY RESOURCES

Click on the plus icon ➕ found in the bottom left corner of each spread to open additional teacher resources.

- Download and print the book's quizzes and activities
- Access curriculum correlations
- Explore additional web applications that enhance the Lightbox experience

LIGHTBOX DIGITAL TITLES
Packed full of integrated media

VIDEOS

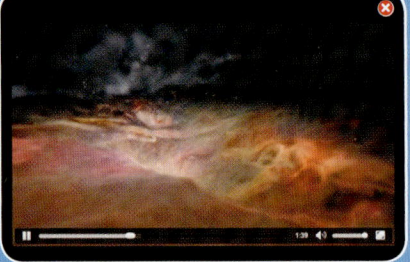

INTERACTIVE MAPS

WEBLINKS

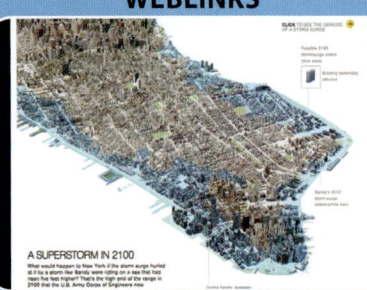

SLIDESHOWS

QUIZZES

OPTIMIZED FOR
✓ **TABLETS**
✓ **WHITEBOARDS**
✓ **COMPUTERS**
✓ **AND MUCH MORE!**

Published by Smartbook Media Inc.
350 5th Avenue, 59th Floor New York, NY 10118
Website: www.openlightbox.com

Copyright © 2016 Smartbook Media Inc.
All rights reserved. No part of this publication may be reproduced, stored in a retrieval system, or transmitted in any form or by any means, electronic, mechanical, photocopying, recording, or otherwise, without the prior written permission of the publisher.

Library of Congress Control Number: 2015942599

ISBN 978-1-5105-0104-1 (hardcover)
ISBN 978-1-5105-0105-8 (multi-user eBook)

Printed in the United States of America in Brainerd, Minnesota
1 2 3 4 5 6 7 8 9 0   19 18 17 16 15

062015
030615

Editor: Katie Gillespie
Designer: Mandy Christiansen

Every reasonable effort has been made to trace ownership and to obtain permission to reprint copyright material. The publisher would be pleased to have any errors or omissions brought to its attention so that they may be corrected in subsequent printings. The publisher acknowledges Getty Images and iStock as its primary image suppliers for this title.

24 Animals of North America